AND THIS HOUSE IS ONLY A NEST

And This House is Only a Nest

JOSE OSEGUERA

WAYFARER BOOKS
BERKSHIRE MOUNTAINS, MASSACHUSETTS

WAYFARER BOOKS
WWW.WAYFARERBOOKS.ORG

Published in 2024 (TRADITIONAL TRACK) by Wayfarer Books
Cover Design and Interior Design by Connor L. Wolfe
Cover Illustrations © Loutje Hoekstra
TRADE PAPERBACK 978-1-956368-89-5
EBOOK 978-1-956368-91-8

10 9 8 7 6 5 4 3 2 1

Look for our titles in paperback, ebook, and audiobook wherever books are sold.
Wholesale offerings for retailers available through Ingram.

Wayfarer Books is committed to ecological stewardship.
We greatly value the natural environment and invest in conservation.

PO Box 1601, Northampton, MA 01060

860.574.5847 | info@homeboundpublications.com

HOMEBOUNDPUBLICATIONS.COM & WAYFARERBOOKS.ORG

for Nicole,

Gio and Luna

Dedication

Thanks to Daniel Overberger, Voltaire Tiñana, David Sannerud, Marco Rodriguez, Steve Martin, Winnie Ocean, Myrto Efstratiou, Cory Bilicko, José Hernández Díaz, Allan Smorra, Gordon Grice, Jason Taksony Hewitt, Judith Estanislao Campbell, Lindsay Armstrong Vance, Adam Bowling, Lina Ogolla, Vivian Taslakian, Mom and Paul, Pedro and Eric, Nadia and Chris, Dad and Mari, Rita and Joe Gyomber, Joe Mendel (who always asked when my next book was coming out), my family, friends and WordPress followers for their generosity, support and love.

My deepest gratitude to Dorsey Craft for her editorial support and Loutje Hoekstra for her beautiful artwork.

In loving memory of Rigoberto Ramírez Marrón

Acknowledgments

Grateful acknowledgment is made to the editors of the following journals, magazines and anthologies, where earlier versions of these poems previously appeared:

About Place Journal: "From Where I Stand"

Avatar Review: "Dime cómo te llamas"

Bending Genres: "Not Because They Hate Us"

Catamaran: "He used to ride horses," "Where the Music Comes From"

Chautauqua: "Chestnut Sun"

Dream Noir Magazine: "Tiny, Unfeeling Things"

Drunk Monkeys: "The Lord's Supper Reenacted by Piñatas Stuffed with Boiled Beans"

Emrys Journal: "Any Shape You Are"

Free State Review: "Small Song in My Chest"

Ginosko Literary Journal: "A Curl of Severed Hair"

great weather for MEDIA: "Gotas de Sangre"

Hal Prize Contest: "Time to Leave the Room Where I've Been Growing Hair from My Face"

Maudlin House: "19 at 12:49 p.m."

Meat for Tea: "As if rivers ran in his heart," "El Michoacano," "Hot Water Soup," "Luciano's Dream"

North Dakota Quarterly: "How the Body Can Be a Sky to Hold the Stars"

Prism Review: "Dad's Folks Used to Hit Him When He Was a Kid," "All the Seed in the World Won't Grow You a Forest," "Without A Trace of Her in Him"

Relief: "One Day I Too Will Wear Stars"

Río Grande Review: "My son is starting to recognize faces," "He Sleeps between Her Breasts"

Sky Island Journal: "Son Para Todos Aquellos Que Son o Fueron Hijos del Sol"

Sonora Review: "Ode to the Dodgers, Ode to Bruce Lee"

Sport Literate: "Hey, Hey, What Can (Jorge) Rodriguez Do"

Stoneboat: "Der Jungenfänger von Nimmerland"

The Main Street Rag: "Apples Come from Washington"

The McNeese Review: "Hats Off to (Marcelino) Bernal"

The Piltdown Review: "If It Were Not So"

Wilderness House Lit Review: "No Pabulum Ever After," "My Mirror No More"

Contents

Sinew

Dear child, you must understand that your home is not here...
and this house where you have just been born is only a nest.

—*from Daily Life of The Aztecs, by Jacques Soustelle*

BONE

If It Were Not So

My Father's house has many rooms.
—John 14:2

As kids, we jumped on Grandpa's sinkhole,
plywood-lined, dandruff-sporing bed
and wore his chamber pot as a hat:
running and screaming,
breaking his things,
gouging his drawers,
silenced by black and white TV blaring
infomercials and you-are-not-the-father chatter,
inhaling the energy bill to the studs.

This unbridled mischievousness never made him
as angry as when he first taught me
how to tie my shoelaces—
the experience of a sage,
dexterity of a giant,
the patience of a kitchen timer
two ticks from wringing itself mad:

"Grab the damn things
and form two loops;
hitch the holes together,
yank them and jerk the knot
as tight as you can.

I wanted to do it right
because the only thing that pleased him
was to never have to repeat himself.
He hated this more than sumbitch guests
who came to drink his water and flush his toilets.

To him, there were only three ways of doing things:
the right way;
the wrong way;
and his way.
His way superseded the right way,
whether it was shoe-tying or construction,
because if he *was* wrong,
he'd simply brush off the doubting stares of onlookers,
grab his hammer, and rip out a wall of sheetrock
and clobber another one in its place
just to show us that where he was
was where we needed to be,
all without wiping his beaded temples
or scratching his balding, gray head.

El Michoacano

or (The man from where Mexico was born)

Pictures weren't his friends;

wrinkles seesawed his cheekbones

long before his hair turned—

silver, ash, granite—

as white as the shirts Grandma pulled

from the soapy washboard and vat,

which came home to her grimed with work.

He was the enemy of anything that made anyone laugh:

quiet.

Grandpa didn't give away his smiles frivolously;

you had to catch him off guard

and compare people he disliked to farm animals.

As opposed to Dad's father,

who prodded me away because the mere sight of me

reminded him that he was old.

Mom's dad didn't care what we called him:

abuelo, abuelito, abuelititito.

It didn't matter;

he'd never let you know

whether he was happy with you or not,

or if he liked you because you were his kids' kid,

or because you kind of looked like him, but not really.

You could rest assured
in one of the six rooms of his solid brick,
steel rebar, concrete house—
an oven during the day, an ice cube at night—
that it was all the same to him:
all cows looked alike.

He'd even curse loudly at himself in the early morning
for coming down with the hammer
on his finger or burning his calloused thumb
with a tortilla directly on a burner grate,
"The charcoal cleans your teeth," he'd say
and crunch on a jalapeño whole.

Grandpa had his father Jesús's gaze—
his black and white portrait hung in the living room—
eyes like rain clouds, heavy
with something they could never rain.

My classmates refused to look at him
daguerreotype-casting Grandpa as evil
as they passed my show-and-tell picture
in a circle like a game of hot potato;
afraid that it would devour their souls.

6

Apples Come from Washington

Sometimes he would slice apples with a knife
he had sharpened only moments
before he fed a slice of white flesh into his mouth.

The blade grazed his lips,
as the fruit's spumy cider
reservoired at the corners of his mouth.
It made Mom nervous because
Grandpa seemed to be biting into the labored metal.

"And when has Pepe gone to the harvest?"
he asked her after his dentures
chewed every drop of juice out
the bruised rinds he swallowed.

As he carved the red sphere
into an hourglass of stem and seeds,
the gray in his once-blue eyes
opaqued as the dust on the apple I held:
dirt, finger oils, wax and tears
of men who missed homes that had grown
accustomed to not having them around.

Ten years after his death, Mom would dream of him,
sleeping in abandoned cars, young and strong—
looking up at stars gleaming too far to show the way back home.

His low wages and elevated stomach
not worthy of tasting even the fruit that rotted off the trees
because that was where juice came from:
raw poison green, unripened, coated in pesticides
not yet gassed or processed off the conveyor belt;
his hands blackened, blistered by the sun,
working other men's fields;
on nights when solitude's cold
sliced through the vapid heat of cheap liquor
that wasn't the warmth of his wife.

He wiped his mouth and took another bite;
I wasn't sure if he was smiling
or wincing from the tartness
dancing on his jaw hinges.

As the sweet nectar worked its way past
his loosely upholstered neck,
elevator Adam's apple,
and protruding clavicle—
a heaving Botticelli crucifix—
I gripped the apple and ate it in silence
thinking on what the point of literacy was
if I couldn't see Grandpa's inability to read.

He Used to Ride Horses

(or, el bracero que si te quiso de a deveras / the laborer that loved you so true)

> *Nothing disturbs them now. Doomed to be idle, to haul no cart or*
> *wagon, wear no bridle. Soul is the issue of so strict a fate. Serene*
> *now, superhuman, they crop their field.*
> *—from "The Horses" by Jorge Guillén, translated by Richard Wilbur*

On the day they took him to the hospital, Grandpa Pedro fell hard
as if a shooting star had struck the orange tree
under which he secretly smoked bud to relieve the pain
from the time he slipped in our shower.
Mom and I knew he would die soon,
both told ourselves, never to one another: "he probably won't."

When I got to the waiting room, my aunt Chabela, Grandpa's oldest daughter,
was standing there— white, bald face— looking away from the family.

"You know," she finally said, "he used to ride his horse—
when he was young— fast, very fast down a hill.
It was so loud that it sounded like a rainstorm hitting the dirt.
All his kids used to come out to see him,
but I was too afraid to look."
In the glassy sheen of her eyes, I could see his:
they didn't merely share the same gaze;
she had her father's eyes.
Her stifled whimpers were like Grandpa's when he used to yelp "ay ya yay!"
as in the refrain of a *corrido* anytime he sat down or got up.

I was ashamed to admit that the memory of his pain still made me laugh,
so I pictured instead the flash of life in him
from a week before when we walked to the corner store
to buy his favorite bread— Entenmann's coconut crunch donuts.
Their Fozzie Bear complexion served as his nightcap
accompanied by a tall glass of milk filled to the brim.
He'd eat them in pairs, frugal even in pleasure.

At the store, we walked straight to the baked goods aisle
where he stacked four rectangular boxes in the shopping cart
as neatly as hay bales, and then back to the checkout line.

As the cashier scanned the items,
Grandpa pulled out money from a blue paisley bandana
as he did back in Mexico,
when he bought a young horse that no one had ever ridden.
The bills were crumpled and worn like his Levi's—
spangled with Birdcatcher spots of paint and bleach.
He handed her the tender gently
as if it would crumble in her hands like a delicate pastry.
The woman at the register stared at one of the bills
and then at Grandpa and back at the bill
as if she were trying to find a resemblance
between his wrinkles and receded hairline and Washington's.

I placed his bread in two plastic bags as he adjusted his *sombrero*
and outstretched his hands towards me.
I knew that all he wanted was to embrace the weight of something
that made him feel useful, to burden his body with work again.

I licked my index finger and peeled away two plastic bags
and shook them until they inflated like rumbling thunder.
I placed a box of Entenmann's in each
and handed him the translucent sacks.

As we walked home, his arms swung listlessly like two freshly braided ropes;
long, thin, but strong enough to tame a wild horse.
Sweat dripped down the waddles of his neck
from the sweatband of his yellow Stetson,
yellowing deeper with every drop.

As we neared the house, I remembered Mom once telling me
that Grandpa always smelled of sweat and dirt and work;
she used to look forward to resting her head on his shoulder
and run her fingertips on the tanned wrinkles
cross-hatched on the nape of his neck.
Though work-withered and rough,
his hands were gentle on her cheek
like a fire that burns the firewood but warms the hearth.

Death's thrumming hooves
bathed my back like a gentle rain
when I saw Grandpa lying unconscious in his room that night.
Though he wasn't going to break this stallion,
I couldn't look away, and for an instance,
I swear I could see him galloping bareback on Lucero—
a horse as indomitable as him—
drunk on aguardiente, his little girl in one arm
and colt mane in his other hand.

Gotas de Sangre

(Blood Drops)

When you're little, you only hear or see things
but you don't really know what they mean,
as when Grandpa stared at the side of his house—
his eyes impenetrable, bloodshot with dense, thick roots—
walls dripping red, defaced by the wounded petals
I ripped from his favorite tree— *su granado*—
and he didn't react the way I thought he would.

Work, work, work
and work was all he knew—
it was his music—
and when he wasn't working,
he was working on getting more work.

The few times I ever saw him off his feet
were in his garden, watching the plants
as they grew the way they grew;
making sure we didn't rip
the flowers off the pomegranate,

and write our names in long distorted striplings
on the stucco's bumpy white,
under the window where Grandma
scolded the cranky wives of La Sánchez Taboada:

"Ain't nobody gonna love my kids
the way he loves them."

Grandpa placed a hand on his waist,
and reached out to the shrub with the other.
He stripped one of its many arms;
the sapling bled sap:

"I hit you," he said, "so that it hurts and you learn,
because those motherfuckers out there,
won't hurt you; they'll kill you."

Although he wasn't my father, or my father's father,
that day, his grace broke my skin,
bleeding through shirts for a week.
I hated him: the way he seemed to be in a bad mood,
even when he was happy,
or the way he spoke, straightforward and simple-hearted.
Most times, he wouldn't say anything—
listening to sad songs to cheer himself up
as he drank a concoction of cinnamon tea,
beer, and sugarcane liquor—
but when he said something, he'd do it.

When he lacked the strength
to speak or breathe— his eyes taped shut
because they wouldn't close—
and his veiny hands rolled off the hospital sheets,
before he died, as cracked pomegranates—
beautiful, purple, delivered—
open for birds to eat out of,
the aftertaste of all his lessons
flourished in me as I saw the strongest man I knew
finally enjoy the fruits of rest.

The gashes he branded me with
grew branches and leaves
that healed beyond my body,
always seeking the light:
the bittersweetness in every drop
of pomegranate blood.

Son Para Todos Aquellos
Que Son o Fueron Hijos del Sol

(Song For Those Who Are or Were Children of the Sun)

Ismael, *mi bien*, you can't change the past

the same way you can't change a man,

especially not one who, as Grandpa Pedro, bore a wiry frame

dense with utility muscle from his work as a farmer and *bracero*.

I remember one time he stood quiet in the kitchen

burning a fresh corn tortilla on the range's grate—

because he liked to eat things that had crunch—

as he listened to his sons reminisce about the times

a guy from church— who'd also been in jail with my dad—

was calling me and my cousins *pendejos* for being so bad at soccer.

"What else did he call you?" one of them asked.

The scent of char filled my eyes

when Grandpa cleared his throat and said "Shut up already."

He allowed the maize moon to eclipse

the blue sun on the grease-coated white stove.

Whether it was the smoke from his lunch

or the fire that flared from his large nostrils,

the sound was sucked out of the kitchen.

Ismael, *mi bien*, you can't change words once spoken
as you can't change he who spoke them.
Yet silence is an open-ended sentence
that can be completed as easy as it is for other people,
who think that little boys stay little, to call them
hijo de puta, hijo de hombre, hijo de la mañana, hijo de la chingada,
hijo de tu derrengada madre, hijo de lo malo, hijo del odio, hijo del peor,
hijo de todo y, a la vez, hijo de nadie.

Ismael, *mi bien*, we are not who we think or are told we are;
for, in the end, are we not the children of those who shape us—
those who take what was wrought, including the rot—
and not necessarily of those who made us?
We are gifts to our parents; we are of them, but don't belong to them.
For, to whom does the moon owe its strength:
to its mother Earth from whom she was ripped away,
or the sun who shares her brilliance
and reveals her adopted daughter's scars,
a beauty that is truer than light itself?

Ismael, *mi bien*, you are a descendant of Grandpa Pedro,
the Israel of our family, he who wrestled with angels and demons—
most of which were his own— to keep his family safe,
even if it meant defending his grandchildren from his children.

"Why didn't you say anything?" Grandpa asked his young sons.
"Why didn't you stand up for them?"
Grandpa bit into his opened-face taco—
muddied with refried beans and a snowfall of cotija—
and looked out the kitchen window, into the front patio
where the first house he built once stood.
He took his time to chew, as he did with everything else,
and turned to my cousin and me.
"The next time that sonofabitch calls you that," Grandpa said,
as his light eyes pierced directly into the organ that beat
whenever others hurt those he loved,
"tell him: shut the fuck up, motherfucker. You don't call me that."

Ismael, *mi bien*, my brother, my younger self,
you might not be my son in name,
but because we are both his, we are each other's,
and in the ancestral home Grandpa Pedro built for us in our veins,
we too can have the courage to leave anything behind
to find and be what we were meant to be.

MUSCLE

Dime cómo te llamas

(Tell Me Your Name)

> *... y te dire quién eres.*
> *—Spanish Proverb*

In Mexico, first-born males
carry their names as they do their crucifixes:
heavy and golden on the nape of their neck.
So, you don't simply have one person
named *Little Bastard Jr.* or *Yet another Bastard III*;
you get a bundle of *Little Bastards*
named after the 'Grand Master Bastard'—
the only one who can never
remember who you are,
defeating the whole purpose
of even having a name.

The desire for your son
to bear your father's name,
and his father's name—
which was his father's
youngest brother's name who died at 21—
becomes so great that
birthing is nothing
more than a game in this perverse botany—
one that requires the scrotums to be as virile
as the wombs fertile:

it's War of the Roses without the war, or the roses,
but all the casualties and hostages.

"Hey, you!" becomes a more
civilized way of distinguishing
one person from the rest
of their similarly named cousins and uncles.
Any arborist would take one
look at this family tree— its roots, seed and soil—
and deem its long branches ripe for firewood

The ancient tradition of genealogical nomenclature
is a lesser crime against humanity—
a misdemeanor at best—
it's public urination marking one's territory,
a branding,
a form of physical,
living, breathing graffiti:
a curse.

The Lord's Supper Reenacted
by Piñatas Stuffed with Boiled Beans

And When Did You Last See Your Father?
by William Yeams, oil on canvas (1878)

The thing Dad hated most was when my siblings and I
misbehaved in church: "Just wait 'til we get to the car,"

was what kept me awake during the long, balmy Sunday morning sermons
flanked by boring people with bad breath and moldy air

sifting through furry vents, sitting on benches upholstered over 50 years before—
a breeding ground for chewed gum, crumbs and dried up moths.

On the ride home, he'd always ask: "Do you know why I'm going to hit you?"
This formality was as unnecessary as the act of going to church in the first place:

my sin that day was taking the Eucharist, Jesus's last meal
before He was fitted for His homecoming dress—Palestine's version

of Sadie Hawkins dance where the sinners courted sin—
sip and nibble of sacramental grape juice and Saltine crackers

to heal my squealing guts, as dogs made of twisted balloons.
No better than Adam, I chose in the face of desire

to break my father's heart, to embarrass him in front of people
he hated but wanted to convince he was good by placing

the forbidden apple core on his head as its cider ran down his face.
In truth, in truth, most of the time, he wouldn't even hit me.

We'd get home, and he'd go back to weaseling money out of Mom
and squandering it on things that were smokable or fit in a syringe,

on what wasn't bread. The little money he made came from
selling our family's things: Mom's jewelry, TV and VCR,

my Pokémon card collection, and letting his friends "borrow"
my social security card or asking me to pee in a cup for his buddy,

"Just this one time," he promised. "Don't be stupid. Don't you know
I can give you a lot of money?" he'd say to try to entice me

to give him these things. But like Jesus, who relinquished
his mutilated body on the cross—His blood smeared on His sweaty,

sun-burnt skin, glistening like butter on toast—I too was a boy
who would always forgive his wicked father and pay for his sins.

The few times Dad would hit me, he'd do it without saying a thing—
quick and dry like a Roman flogging. The sound of finely-crafted

Mexican calf leather stone-skipping red on tightly squeezed flesh
rippled in my ears, dousing my spine with shivers. The afterburn

embraced me from thorny crown to nailed foot as I knew
we'd have communion afterward and his interest in me, resurrected.

So, sometimes, especially on Sunday mornings, I'd sin on purpose.

Tiny, Unfeeling Things

Mom dug her long,
self-manicured fingernails
into my hand, dragging me
into the dentist's office,
to patch the holes on my teeth
bored by Frosted Flakes I used to eat
for breakfast, lunch, and dinner.
The cavities were wider than the gaps
between my teeth, the ones she wouldn't
allow the pedodontist to brace
because they were like hers.

These crevasses felt as familiar
as the bite in the words
she'd scream through clenched jaws;
I mourned my bone wounds as the dentist's assistant
prepared my mouth and numbed the gums—
cheeks tranquilized dead.
The skull chunk ripped out by the dentist
left my body cracked and in pain for hours later.

I wonder if that was when I first unlearned to laugh for no reason
and began gnashing my joy in my molars,
tucking it away safely for a day
when I could allow it to seep out of me
like a mouthful of blood through a smile.

These tiny, unfeeling things
I ground and ground,
little by little every night, like a prayer
destroying tissue with the best of intentions.
The sound of her pain in my head
was an uninvited guest dragging its mangled body
against every surface, one who didn't want to leave,
not because it had grown accustomed to me
but because it no longer knew where it was from
or where it was going.

It hurt to smile—
even when unaided by Mom pinching my back fat—
and the soft cotton wads stuffed deep,
packed tight in my cheeks
soaking the oozing exit wounds
did very little to help.

19 at 12:49 p.m.

In Spanish, the word mama translates to "nurse" or to "fuck with" if you place emphasis on the first syllable— a single word to mean and be the mean of the two. It can also stand for "mother" if the stress is placed on the second.

However, the stress fell on her first, her maiden voyage into motherhood, an uncharted excursion on a vessel kneaded of virgin soil whet with love-promises, kilned into something meant to float, but instead hardened from waiting and wading, weighing her relationship down into a sea of diary pages that, day after day, weak after weep,

capsized into an abandoned ship, a journal rotted with dust where she seldom wrote about the few important things that happened to her: meeting a guy on a summer church retreat in 1984; her early February wedding in 1985; and later that year, 19 years old and three months, the birth of her son.

She'd often drown in the vast ocean between the few English words she'd managed to learn and those she knew not the meaning of, the ones she read as if they were in Spanish: son, a single syllable word that carried

the full weight of accent and meaning: a "sound" spoken deep within her womb; a "song" she liked, but couldn't remember the words to; a "rumor" that she was already late by the time her "first time" slid the ring on her. In her Tijuana dialect, the word was anything but a simple homonym to the heat and light you could easily cloud from your eyes with your fingers.

In her mami's house, she was never given any proper lesson on men and their ways, especially not by her papá—silent and hard-faced as a potato, unmoved and uptight like a pope. Yet, how much water can be held with the palm of your hands before the boat starts to sink?

If she were to die today, her log would be the only thing

left behind to keep her legacy afloat— stranded letters fingered on sand pages washed away by currents of her own making. I wonder how many times my name appears in that ragged thing, or the term she uses to refer

to herself or in relation to me. Not madre, which is to a mother what Homo sapiens is to a living, breathing person who cast away part of herself to have you; it's a name given— prescribed taxonomy— to qualify the flesh, not the scars.

Ama, on the other hand, means "to love" if used as a verb and stress is placed on the first "a"; as a noun, it means "mistress or landlady," both of which she's been to me, in her body and in the places she's called home.

¡Amá! A single word to raft a single woman's mistake and mercy to me; it's the embodiment of "mommy"— a name earned amidst life's storms and shipwrecks— if you place the stress, as she's always reminded me to do so, on the second.

Hats Off to (Marcelino) Bernal

We jumped out of our seats
as high as our Nike Airs allowed us,
and yelled Viva México
in spite of being reprimanded
by our teacher not to speak
Spanish in the classroom,
even though it was technically recess.

"El pinche indio Bernal
scored a hell of a goal
on those fancy, cocky-ass Italians,"
kept running through my head,
neck to neck with my adrenaline
as the two Italian defenders
who couldn't get there in time
to prevent his shot.

Marcelino's mullet flapped on
the nape of his neck
like black-crested caracara feathers,
his white jersey thrashed loosely
under his arms as eagle's wings:
our hero,
our cock in the fight.

I was sure that had his teammates
not tackled him,
Bernal would have flown out
of Robert F. Kennedy Memorial Stadium
into the blue skies of Washington DC,
over the Lincoln Memorial,
and into heaven like Elijah.

The English-speaking commentators
were speechless—
jaw-dropped as they saw a prince
from our tribe be marvelous, divine—
so quiet that our teacher was afraid
that all of our jumping around
had somehow broken the television.

They couldn't describe what they had seen:
a flyover country scaling Olympus
and landing a jab on Zeus himself?
Had these journalists found it
worthwhile to research Marcelino's stats—
butchering his name
as if reading it for the first time—
they would've known that
that 5-foot-11-inch man of bronze skin
from Tepic, Nayarit
had a rocket launcher of a right leg.

As dumbfounded as they were,
they deemed the phenomenon an error
on the part of the Italians—
a fortunate rebound,
an act of voodoo chichimeca
rather than a feat of athletic ingenuity—
their analytical minds
couldn't understand what
three bean-and-tortilla fed
fourth-graders knew in their hearts;
something their aunts and uncles
never allowed them to forget:
"Nobody ever gives nothing to people like us.
That's why we need to celebrate
all the small victories
because who knows if we'll ever hit it big."

We crossed our fingers,
held our breaths,
and prayed a Hail Mary
for every minute of play
until we turned blue all over.
We were prepared to die
on the field along with the Mexican team.

The school bell rang,

our teacher switched off the TV

and flicked on the lights.

The sweaty chatter and sneaker screeches

of our classmates flooded the room.

We rubbed our eyes

adjusting to the incandescence

and wiping tears of joy

for the men in whose faces we saw our own.

We knew that after the goal

Mexico would probably get trampled on the field

because there were still 30 minutes left of the game.

But maybe, just maybe

a goddamn, sumbitch indio

would get away, for once,

with more than he could ever dream of.

Hey, Hey, What Can (Jorge) Rodriguez Do

in a situation in which he knows he's going to lose even before he's lost?
As when he and the rest of the Mexican soccer team
were on the cusp of winning the round of 16 match in the 1994 World Cup.
That summer, I learned that Mexicans
must like to suffer because they sure as hell lost a lot.

My hands were sweaty as Rodriguez
placed the ball on the penalty spot;
my uncles were quiet, choking the blood out of their fists
thinking about the through pass
that pierced right by Rodriguez
during the game which left his teammate alone
to defend the goal against Bulgaria's Hristo Stoichkov—
known in Europe as "The Knife"—
who stabbed the ball with his left foot
and plunged his strike into the goalkeeper's net:
1 to 0 the score with a whole game to go.

Rodriguez walked dejected toward the edge of the penalty box
as a man whose soul had vacated him in life,
a wraith fading in the New Jersey summer
before a roaring crowd of 71,000 in Giants Stadium.

As we stared at him, he stared at the match ball
as if it were made out of crystal,
a magic orb that reflected a wispy moustache that stuck out
and draped over the brim of his upper lip.
Did he see a version of himself different
from the solitary player whose legs were shaking?
Or a confident man who sought a valor that didn't know when to quit
or when enough was enough,
that wanted to win just to *win*,
or, hopefully, because he knew there was a little boy
lost somewhere in Los Angeles
who needed Mexico to be victorious, just this time?

The weight of 92 million Mexican hearts
beat hotter than the sun on Rodriguez's shoulders
as he geared up in the locker room,
slid his legs into white shorts and rolled up red socks,
and draped on his chest
the inescapable heartbreak of *la verde*.

When the referee blew the whistle,
the stunted organ in my chest began to sweat icicles.
Rodriguez ran toward the ball—
5 foot 4 inches of dynamite—
with the grace of one running out
of a burning building onto grass that

Pope John Paul II would celebrate Mass
and baptize with October rain a year later.
Rodriguez's foot went through the ball as a phantom limb,
the immolated feet that he'd inherited from Cuauhtémoc, the last Aztec Emperor.

The opposing keeper stifled his shot: no goal.
Three shots, three misses from the Mexican team, the announcer lamented,
more to himself than to the TV audience.
We were all upset when he missed;
I'd never seen my uncles cry,
but after Rodriguez yelled *puta madre* in frustration,
it was the closest I'd ever seen their eyes to tears.

I don't know why, but there's always something that the Mexican athlete lacks,
one of them said, bitter from the taste of defeat in his mouth.
I don't know if it's a lack of desire or strength or balls:
that's really why Mexico will never, ever win a goddamn World Cup.

Rodriguez and the rest of *La Selección*
entered the East Rutherford field
as golden eagles, but left as honey
bees who'd frolicked in grass with lions,
trying to pollinate every single leaf
instead of striving for the golden prize;
crushed under foot before billions of eyes, yet murdered in anonymity
in a stadium where Bulgaria would play two more times:
one in victory, one in defeat.

Der Jungenfänger von Nimmerland

(The Piper from Neverland)

In middle school, my closet
was packed with T-shirts—
hanging portraits of all my dead classmates—
scripted in Lucida Handwriting
their dates of birth dashed
by their dates of death.

On these wearable tombstones,
their chiaroscuro faces stared back
like Mona Lisas del barrio—
cosmic fragments in the ether
of Roscoe Boulevard, visible
through one-hundred percent cotton windows.

When they were living children,
cops saw them as target practice,
and vatos locos as bar examinations
they needed to pass in order to break the law,
to prove— to themselves
and to every good-for-nothing cholo veterano—
that they were real men,
something that their victims would never become.

"Get a size large, fool," my buddy said,
at the school gate before an asphalt altar illuminated
by la Virgen María de Guadalupe jar candles.
"These 3-for-1 pieces of shit shrink like a motherfucker."

There was a finite number of us
that would go on to high school
and I knew my turn would eventually
come to join the game.
If I said "no,"
they'd call me a pussy
and they'd be right. I was.

I wasn't afraid of dying
but of imagining my mother
reliving my murder
every time she washed
the T-shirt with my face on it—
a corpse chicken poxed with exit wounds,
swaddled in body bag-black,
waiting for her eyes
to identify and claim
like an old, corduroy jacket
forgotten at the cleaners.

"I guess you're right," I said,
trading the medium for a large.
"Yeah," my buddy said, "that way we can just flip 'em
over and wear them as undershirts."
He laughed. I didn't, not because it wasn't true,
but rather, because I was taught never
to laugh at those who couldn't hear it.

Out of the 15 shirts that owned me—
textile ghosts gently waving at half-mast—
the one I allowed gravity
to unfold from my hand
wore a face I once knew well.
He had the same smile
as when we sat criss-cross applesauce
on a big alphabet rug in first grade—
I sat between letters J and K, he on L.
When his bottom tooth fell out,
he showed me the gap it left;
its departure, still raw.

Not Because They Hate Us

—after *Tao Te Ching*

I spent prom night
in the school's handball courts playing
pachuco with my friends—
boys trained like dogs to look down,

hands on their head, legs spread—
ricocheting the tiny, atomic-blue
rubber racquetball as hard
as our budding muscles could

off one another's bodies
until our tawny asses and backs—
balmy, but not as wet as our parents'—
turned purplish-Prussian.

Passed down to us
by our fathers, uncles,
older brothers and cousins,
in between jail sentences,

this helped to toughen us up—
a Mexican predilection for pain
or presage for when the time
of our arrests and incarcerations came?

It'd probably be for stealing something
people like us should never be able to afford,
for smoking stuff too hard
even for our growing bodies,

or smoking a fool
for wearing a baseball cap
stitched with the wrong letters,
cholo cuneiform etched forever
black and white on his frigid, brown skin;
cheeks turgid sweet on the cold pavement
for the cops to unwrap like a chocolate.

Watching each other smoke weed
out of a punctured apple—
a heart with two arteries
pumping incense, skunk urine and cider vinegar—

toking vapor until our cheekbones clenched as plums,
we suppressed the red-eyed,
ain't nobody give a shit about us blues;
smoking an apple a day
to keep them fuckers away.

We felt as weightless in the Sun Valley breeze
as the wishes we mushroomed out like genies,
mouths gaped like exit wounds,
the long plumes danced skyward
to twirl as if the moon took them by the hand.

The sound of sirens diffused
in the smog-bruised night sky,
dispersing us into the neighboring homes
starting to yawn their lights on.

The red and blue piercing through our haze
reminded us to run away and hide,
but the fog blurring the streetlights
lifted our chins and led us home
through the still dark;
another day was coming,
and soon everything would be quiet again.

No Pabulum Ever After

When Dad came home from prison,
he cooked for us a special meal:
instant ramen noodles spangled with bits
of desiccated carrots and peas,
sopping over spongy bits of nacho cheese Doritos,
and spattered with red hot sauce.
Mom smiled at the plate Dad served her
the same way she did at the church people
whenever they'd say they were praying for her husband.

Mom took bite after bite, sometimes swallowing without chewing,
never once breaking eye contact with her plate,
not even as she took deep swigs from her water glass.
She had finished her food before any of us
and raised her hand to her face to dampen an inaudible burp.

She hoped each morsel would stifle
the cavity that had grown and ground her tired voice
to a haematid asking, "Why is he back? Is he here to stay this time?"
that the bland, grease sliding down her esophagus
still hadn't been able to.

Mom stared at us as we chewed the abscess rife on our plates
and reprimanded me for asking disgustedly, "What's this?"
"Shut up and eat it," she hissed.

"It's okay," Dad replied with a chuckle.
"It's pizza, or, at least, what my cellmate and I
used to make with what we had around
whenever we missed the outside."

What about when Mom craved him, her pie whole again?
What was left for her to use when her soulmate broke his promise
of sticking together until the end?
I wondered if the taste of this insipid meal—
one that was supposed to bring us all together—
reminded her of their first kiss or their last.

As Dad wore his old clothes and held us hostage in his affection,
Mom went into the kitchen for seconds,
scraping every last noodle onto her plate
as if eating it all would also eat her man's sin.

She partook of this first supper as if it were the last,
a renewed covenant, not because she thought it was good,
but rather, because she thought it'd be good for her children
to see the man in baggy, stale clothes as one
who loved to spend hours in the kitchen,
rather than the man we'd heard so many prayers about.

Without a Trace of Her in Him

Dad was passed out in the living room
when we got home; the lack of light made it
indecipherable to tell where the couch began and he ended.
Mom's face was difficult to see in the dark,
her long, black tresses blotted her pale skin,
but the faint glimmer in her eyes, a silent prayer,
was distant like two shining cities
on peakless hills, her youth eroded;
the plateaus of what was left to live on.

"Go to your room and read the Bible," she said,
as the tears that had been welling up in the car,
two windshields saturated with rain,
finally released into the feathered paths of her crow's feet.

"You don't need a dad like *your* dad," Mom said on our way back from vespers.
"*Your* dad is Jesus, the best dad anyone could ever want."
"But Jesus never had kids," I replied.
"He didn't even have a girlfriend."
"Shut up! Don't take the Lord's name in vain," Mom replied.
"The scripture is sacred... "
yeah, yeah, I knew the sacred out of that thing—
from old Methuselah to New Jerusalem:
God makes boy and girl;
boy falls for girl;

girl feeds naughty fruit to boy,
and they fuck up the world
until God makes another boy— a *special* boy—
and breaks him to unfuck it up.
I doubted that Special Boy
would ever want to marry a woman who only
spoke the truth in hushed tones.

"Besides," Mom continued, "your dad is trying his best."
It always surprised me to hear her
defend him even amidst her sermons
on why nothing he did
was "sacred" in her eyes.

It was her way of patching together
the home she'd always wanted.
But how do you mend one who refuses to give up
and runs to church, her sanctuary,
and hiding place, a Jerusalem above
where sins could be cashed-in for mercy?

Mom and Dad fought so often, about so many things
it was hard to imagine a time when they had been just amicable,
let alone happy and in love:
a brief moment when she'd ask him to do something,

and he'd actually do it without any underbreath commentary
or blame for asking him in the first place,
or question the tone she'd *intentionally* use,
not to get him to do the thing she wanted him to do, but to humiliate him.

This was their bliss— to hurt one another—
their normal, better or worse,
their happily ever after, their I do.

Though I couldn't see the Tabernacle of God in tiny script,
the only thing I learned how to read that night was her:
the dewy, infinitesimal system of emotions she cataloged
with great care behind her auburn irises.

Yet, I continued to read the Word
to see if I could find something to tell her,
a Zion to give to this prayer warrioress,
my bride of Christ.

Hot Water Soup

"At your age, I could find my own food and cook it,"
Dad would say when we'd tell him we were hungry.
Mom's response to his parental wisdom:
"Well, that's because your dad and his brothers
were raised like animals."

The few times he *did* cook,
Dad used to heat up water in a pockmarked pot,
big enough for a single mug.

"Why don't you make enough soup
so that your kids can also eat?" Mom said
as the soft-boiled water's chlorinated rank
softened the acrid track scent of metal
scraping against a rusted burner grate.

"It's not soup," Dad said
and poured the liquid into his cup.
"It's just water."

He blew on the porcelain lip
and slurped with a stare as empty as his stomach.

"Well, at least warm up enough for them too," Mom said.
She was like a bitch who'd rather eat her puppies
than watch them go without food,
damned if she didn't try to make her thin paycheck
spread as far as spilt water.

As Mom walked towards the door,
Dad placed the cup on the counter
and embraced her as carefully as one would
hold a nearly full receptacle,
ready to spill equal measures of love and hate.
There was no hug or kiss from her end,
just a stranger embracing another stranger,
a mop, vacant stoneware
and not a woman who'd carried his children
on three separate occasions.

As they stood there,
all they hated, loved and hoped for
was as visible as the arsenic and phosphorus
caked on the sides of the charred pot.
She dug her claws in his skin,
as she did into every word she spoke to him,
and walked towards the door.

"So, I guess you guys probably want some too,"
Dad said after he heard Mom close the garage
and slam shut the car door.

We drank a lot of tap water soup,
not for the taste, but rather,
because it made our bellies pop-out
and our guts feel warm inside and out:
the cocktail of minerals wouldn't kill
the hunger, but it'd drown the growling, our flaws,
and deliver us into a torpor that felt nice
until Mom got back from work.

Dad's Folks Used to Hit Him When He Was a Kid

—after *Fiona Staples and Brian K. Vaughan's "Saga, Chapter Fifty Four"*

His mom used to send him and his siblings
to Tijuana to stay with their grandma for months at a time.
Dad would tell me how he used to play soccer
in the streets of barrio Sánchez Taboada,
off Andrómeda street where a galaxy
of kids would emerge from dark, lopsided houses
and run onto the dilapidated dirt-paved roads.
There, the rules of the game didn't matter—
no tally was ever kept—
because they played for fun:
the real goal was to score their knees, get dirty,
and shed who they were told to be.

Dad's heart wasn't forged in the streets,
but he was as fatherless as if he belonged there:
bastards of fathers who never loved them;
children of men who were never taught
the roles and duties of a man;
boys raised to be men by women overwhelmed
with too much responsibility.

All of that didn't matter when they played *fútbol*,
feeling unstoppable, becoming immortal
as the ball rolled between their ankles—
individually, they were defenseless, runty *mocosos*,
but together, they had no need for fathers;
they accepted nothing and rebelled against it all.
All they needed was a ball that rolled,
like a tennis ball or even a golf ball;
hell, they would've played soccer with a ping pong ball.
And if there was nothing to play with,
I'm sure they would've plucked a star from the sky
and juggled it on their heads and thighs.

They played endlessly, and chased the sun into the night,
when the bright sphericality of a full moon
gave them enough light to play until their limbs gave out.
They ran as if chased by a pack of rabid dogs,
faster than their lungs could oxygenate their depleted bodies,
getting their fill of fighting and making up
over chilled bottles of cane sugar Coca-Cola.

Dad would go to bed tired, but unable to sleep—
wiggly feet under Mamá Chole's crocheted blankets—
his heart pumped as if a drummer were pounding
a mallet against his sternum.

The sound of the beat reminded him
of all the things they had laughed about,
how their ribs ached so much they didn't feel hunger
for the drumsticks and rolls they couldn't afford
or the pain from the grooves welt on his skin
struck by his grandpa's belt buckle.

A paradiddle of the flesh
to remind Dad that his mom would rather hold his dead body
out of pity and compassion
than see him become the man she loved.

Ode to the Dodgers, Ode to Bruce Lee

Empty your mind, be formless, shapeless like water.
Now, you put water into a cup, it becomes the cup.
Now, water can flow or it can crash.
Be water.

—Bruce Lee

1.

When the lineup of prisoners first filed into the visiting room,
I picked out Dad by the beard, patchy like the El Cariso baseball fields

in San Fernando. The last time I saw him was ten years before
on the night he was betrayed by undercover cops posing as junkies;

they caught him in a rundown right as he was planning to steal himself home.
"Wow, mijo, you look so big," he said after he hugged me

for a prolonged period of time. "I almost didn't recognize you."

2.

I could still remember the undercover officers that sat in the living room
with my siblings and me as the lead investigator debriefed Mom

in one of the bedrooms. "So, how old are you?" one of the cops asked,
the one that reminded me of Dodgers' first baseman, Eric Karros.

"Twelve," I said after I realized my brother and sister weren't going
to interrupt their carpet-gazing. "Hmmm," he said and crossed his arms,

partially embracing his belly. He didn't seem interested in questioning me
any further given Dad's already full count: 3 kids, 2 strikes on his record,

and no outs this time around.

3.

The narcs gave Mom a Ziploc bag large enough to fit everything
Dad had been wearing that night: his clothes, brown leather shoes,

and latex gloves. Though they chafed my inner thighs,
I wore his boxers to school the following week and for months thereafter:

white, cratered with moth holes, patterned with the New York Mets' mascot,
Mr. Met.

4.

I felt a phantom itch near my knees as Dad and I took a seat
at a chair and table bolted to the ground, ensuring the inmates' safety

in the event of a bench-clearing brawl. "Remember when we used to watch
kung fu movies?" he said. "I was thinking about that time you kicked

a tostada out of your brother's hand." He smirked. "Yeah, that was pretty badass."
I smiled at the memory. The blow had been so swift and well-placed

that the petrified tortilla flew across the kitchen, out of my brother's hand—
who continued to hold the outline of a disc for seconds afterward—

landing intact in an ajar drawer. "You remember what he used to say?" Dad said.
"Who? My brother?" I said. "No, Bruce Lee. In that scene where he smacks

his student for focusing on his finger and not at what the finger
was pointing to: the moon."

5.

When the officers left, Mom stayed in her room for what felt like months.
When she came out, her lips were pursed with her fists at her waist

just as Jesus when he was tasked to not let the cup pass from Him, or Lee,
to fight his way up a five-story pagoda filled with martial arts masters,

or the Mets, to clad themselves with blue and orange. She understood
that she'd have to be our leadoff man and clean-up hitter, our coach and umpire.

She sat down beside us and told us Dad wouldn't be around for at least 12 years—
a crooked number for a crooked man. That night, I dreamt Dad and I

were spirits swimming in a river of colostrum inside of Mom's body,
one that satiated our sins, but not our thirst to remember.

6.

One of the inmates was celebrating his birthday, so they gave us all
a slice of cake and coffee with 2% milk. After taking the cup,

Dad gave thanks and said, "You know, I'm glad you took after me,
in looks, I mean. Your Mom's brothers are all short." And as he separated

the frosting from the sponge, the distinction I had made between his role
as a parent and that of my buddy became as insignificant as the distance

between Brooklyn and Queens. "Well," Dad said, pausing to lick
the brown frosting from the plate, "she did breastfeed you as a baby,

so I guess that helped."

7.

Dad's ejection from our home marked the end of a losing season,
one filled with name-calling and bad calls, slides and bruises

from the battery he'd formed with Mom. Before she got up from the couch,
she reached for my hand. I felt a shock as our fingers made contact—

currents of her blood and his short-circuiting my veins—
and I suddenly felt it would've been better for me to have dissolved

into her amniotic fluid, if I hadn't been born.

8.

I left the prison as I once had Dodger Stadium after a 12-inning playoff loss,
trying to rid myself of something that was drowning me from within.

I remember walking into a sea of people flooding every stairwell,
pathway, and sidewalk, where I no longer felt like a person, but a drop.

I stopped crashing into people trying to find an exit and allowed myself
to be borne by the flow. I wanted to be nothing, to be water.

SINEW

Any Shape You Are

(Winner of the Nancy Dew Taylor Award)

Even if you were born a fairy,
with wings as light as whispers—
thin as songs sung in silence—
I'd hold out my pointer finger
as a perch for you to rest,
present my palm flat for you to play,
and cup my hands like a heart for you to sleep.

Even if you grew a mermaid's tail
and hair as long as stories told and retold—
thick and lustrous as secrets kept secret—
I'd caulk all the windows
and brick all the doors— two times two-fold—
turn the chimney into a mortal manhole,
fill our house with saltwater,
and pray to God for gills.

Even if you came into this world
as the smallest litter of all—
a little pussy who yawned like a roar—
I'd love you as fiercely as a tiger
and hunt for all you needed
to grow as strong as a lion.

Even if you hatched out of an egg
and came out a chicken
with speckled feathers for hair
grazing on grass and seed,
I'd buy us a farm where your growing wings
could flap wherever the breeze took you,
and build you a coop big enough for 10 eagles
where we could comfortably roost,
and keep out the wolves
regardless of all the hot air they blew.

Even if you were the moon
and your mom had the biggest bump
anyone had ever seen,
you'd be born magnificent and bright
as the stars from where you came;
we'd hold your hand
and release you, flying high into sky,
far, far away so you couldn't see our tears
glimmering up at you as you watched over us,
wishing you goodnight,
never to hold you in our arms again.

Even if your mom and I were trees
and you a faggot of our branches,
though armless logs we'd be,
you'd make us the gayest parents

as you cried us out of sleep,

for you were the fuel

burning from within us

before your 9-month hibernation began—

back when you were still a wish

and our love for you

ran as deep as gravity's roots.

Even if your body's shape

wasn't that of a humanoid, but instead

you looked like a triangle, rhombus or trapezoid,

we'd find the chicest clothes—

of all colors, patterns and fabrics—

that fit you the best

because you should never

squeeze into molds

made for someone else

that someone else made.

Even if you were more olive than human,

and what I saw of you was a dream,

I'd spend the rest of my life

asleep, combing through my subconscious

as the wind every leaf

brown, yellow, white or green—

the sound of earth's breathing

so we too can breathe—

because I'd always know you were mine.

Even if you're due in May instead of June,
we'll have two hearts—
yours, once one with mine,
now separate but shared—
and with it you'll learn
that we can change the meaning
of the words we use—
to heal or to hurt—
as we can all choose love instead of hate,
not because it's easier,
because whichever you decide to choose
will be who you'll become.

With two minds to think what we please,
to do what is right, know what is fair;
four eyes to see one another
for who we truly are
not who we were told to be—
for what a queer thing it is
to seek out what's different
only to reject what makes us the same.

And one love to share, as we share
with all, the life that we're given.

My son is starting to recognize faces

and mistrust those he doesn't. He can tell the contrast between lights on and off— black and white— but not when I do things for him out of love rather than responsibility or when I do what I don't want to and I do it anyway because he is woven to my bones tighter than sinew.

He hasn't learned to tell time yet, and I've forgotten everything I knew about it: it is suspended, no longer a thing I can spend or waste or use wisely or otherwise; it is divided into the time I'm with him, and the time that I'm not; the moments when I get to be his dad and when I'm just any other man.

His hazel eyes stare at me as if he knew who I was or where I've been or how many scores it took for me to be here with him; they try to dissect the cipher of nonsense dispelled from wry lips that smell of stale green tea— metallic and forgotten— asking questions more mysterious than his life— when a syndrome could confiscate him at any moment— or his birth— with all its miscarriage scares— or his death— unknown yet almost foreseen.

His fontanel billows when he smiles— a water drum pot percussed by an invisible drummer— which, at 3 months, isn't often. The thin membrane inflates as if his heart was too big for his tiny body or his soul— too wild for this world— were trying to escape out of his strawberry-fuzzed crest.

They say that a little bit of your soul leaves the body every time you laugh. Thankfully, nothing I've contorted my facial muscles into has made him that happy: his soul is intact, unwasted, one way in, one way out.

His chest locks up when his temper shrieks awry. It's all part of a nightly game we play called bedtime or, pin the baby on the crib mattress: a challenge of wits, a race to see who can get to the end of theirs last; it's a lot like chess, a pawn and a king with no black or white squares left in between, each with one move to make, both weak— one dispensable, one defensible. It's still early in the game: it's his move and, without admitting defeat, I'm pretty sure I'm the pawn.

Time to Leave the Room Where I've Been Growing Hair from My Face

—after Forrest Gander's "Loiter";
for Joe Gyomber

The hair that shrubs under my nose and ivies under my jaw

and down my neck is long enough to grab,

patchy like my father's— archipelagos

and peninsulas of crabgrass follicles—

thicker at the chin than at the cheeks.

My son submerges his 6-month-old fingers

into the dark mane and grips,

a sharp whisper to my nerve endings:

"Tell me when it hurts,

and then, try to forget about it."

The hair I've been growing on my face

is dry and gnarled but never dead,

stubborn weeds that line his way.

He mouths and soaks the shag—

Christ thirsty for the sponge on the hyssop—

as if he can eucharise their sour wine into mother's milk.

These whiskers are all he knows,
unaware of what or who bathes and dresses him for bed
as Mary Magdalene prepared her Lord's body for resurrection:
I am a pangea whose gaps
he'll have to learn to ignore;
a mass of everything he knows outside the womb,
anamnesis of the time we were once one substance—
he, the vinegar and I, the mother.

Now, as he coos in my arms, we are one again:
an island in this world whose fragments are stable enough
to keep him still while he grows—
all for the moment when he comes alive on his own.

He nestles his head against my beard
and falls asleep within minutes,
minutes that slip their small bodies between ours,
regardless of how close we hold one another;
minutes that leave without saying goodbye;
and though I've nailed down plenty of them in pictures,
they're minutes whose empty husks remind me,
months later, that they'll never return.

As if Rivers Ran in His Heart

We traverse our one-bedroom apartment:
corner to corner, wall to wall, latitude and longitude
we stare at bookshelves caked with our dead skin;

we talk to faces in picture frames;
we stare at each other in mirrors and spoons
and windows and surfaces that take our reflection,
but don't give it back;

we forget that light means day and dark means night,
that walking is a balancing act,
and sleeping, an armistice of sorts.

Your eyes are like the lens of a hidden camera show—
always on, always live—
broadcasting everything I do and say
to the inhabitant in your head
who uses the footage as its basis
for how it should act and speak.

Though you are the smallest unit of humankind,
I envy how much you care and try with all your might
to live and eat and hold your head up when everything
in this inhospitable planet pushes you down.

Our neighbors, annoyed that you cry so much,
don't care that you are still in your raw form—
imperfect little creature hopelessly overwhelmed
by a sea of imperfect souls.

You can take this world for granted,
sleep, and wake up the next day
and the next and the next
only to realize life will never stand still
or allow you to feel right in whatever stage of human you're in.

How you remind me of a flood,
a force that overtakes me,
outpouring onto everything I thought I knew
about the place I thought of as mine—
a cataclysm that signaled the destruction
of the past and the beginning of something better.

All the seed in the world won't grow you a forest

His every wince, scream and tear are a knife
polished soft and sharp;
lodged deep inside my chest,
it plunges into me an immeasurable depth—
between the muscles,
scraping against the ribs,
tickling the heart—
when I see his eyes studying my ways.

He looks like me,
they say and I don't deny it;
he *is* me,
and I *was* him,
yet what answer will I give him
when his wonder punctures my arteries?
When he asks why men are so fucking childish:
why do they want what they can't have
and throw away what is given them?

Its naked metal
cuts through all my layers—
the salvageable, the rotten, the figured-out, the bullshit—

because its unnamed sheen hasn't learned to pretend
only to probe and discover
that whatever he didn't come equipped with
I can do nothing to give him.

He is my possession,
a wound carved in my chest,
a living thing that takes up space—
inheritor of all my worst traits,
reminder of the things I've learned to forget.

I've often mistaken the blood-dripping handle
sticking out of my sternum
for an appendage I grew
after his waxy-blue body
was exhumed from woman
and placed on my skin:

it is a nipple that shivers
and lactates a milk that doesn't nourish
because being a man is sometimes
easier than running away;
his irises, still in flux,
frustrated to tears
look for what he'll never find in my ilk.

A Curl of Severed Hair

—Title from a poem by Algernon Charles Swinburne

The wisps that sprouted like whiskers atop his head
have begun to drape over his ears like a Rubber Soul Beatle
and feather out the back of his neck like a peacock.
They lattice a reddish tapestry—
a perfect ombré coursing from mousy to vulpine—
over his disappearing fontanel,
a cycloptic eyelid sutured shut by its lashes,
joint so that his eyes could see
the world as it's always been,
as it will never be again.

As his brain continues to grow under soft skull,
he calls out to his echo whenever we walk down the stairwell
and looks around the cement crevasse for its reply.
As the siren of his voice fades,
I comb the fuzz mossing over his converging craneal tracery,
and wonder when my fear that, someday,
he might wake up dead will go away:
how much hair and bone will it take to satiate that chasm?

I rub his fontanel with my fingers as one would the flesh of an egg:
I want to enjoy its fragility before
he finds my soft spots, and perforates them
until I'm defenseless to the things I'll have to swallow
as dog hairs floating invisible afloat the surface of a glass of water.

How can I slow down, my heart,

the tectonic motion under his infant acton—

a still place of no give, and no-take—

until our whole beings reverberate at the rate of waves

rippling away from the center of our couch,

our universe,

where stars and planets, black holes and dark matter

were birthed with the selfsame violence living in the very cells

that make the nebulous pigments in his eyes

stare at me as I stroke his hair?

How the Body Can Be a Sky to Hold the Stars

—Title after *Karla Cordero*

The mole that orbited back and forth between his forehead and cheekbone
has finally found sanctuary on his right temple.
It burns bright like a star equidistant from the helix of his ear
and the lateral canthus of his eye—
a distance traveled only by a tearful little dipper.

His eyes, their nebulous steeliness, are my mother's:
strong, brown, unbreakable; hard to read, easily wounded;
silent spheres that turn quickly as the moon from phase to phase,
eyes born to suffer, twin celestial bodies steeled
for the impact of meteorites and space debris.

They smile, though never in photographs,
and laugh with a silence that can only be heard
from afar as the sparkles of intergalactic jewels
that do so without care or inhibition, unaware or burdened by earthly gazes.
The chiaroscuro beneath his eyes is burdened by the phrase,
Mom's refrain: "your son is my new Pepito, my new you;
a new chance to make things right."

He lies in his crib, unfazed, as the orbs inside my head
remember that as bright as she may be,
the moon is nothing but stone with no brilliance of its own—
a mere reflection of the sun— just as my satellites and his

are but mere moons to my mother's Jupiter;
eyes don't produce their own light,
their brilliance and power emanates from the eyes they remind you of,
their cores, cones and rods, as they age, create heavier and heavier elements,
a sorrow that remains in the iris as an afterimage.

But mostly, his eyes remind me of hers when he cries
because light years ago, in a faraway place we once called home,
she used to paint most starless nights with a big dipper full of tears.

My Mirror No More

There's a wolf in us all;

it grows heavy in our bones

as it gently nibbles away

at all that is wild and pure and bare.

At 10 months, you mouth at anything whose will

your soft, long fingers can bend—

the pianist's hands my grandma Chole used to say I had at your age.

Yet from the same litter, we are different:

you were born of chaos and night—

child of earth and love—

and thirst the ocean and the clouds;

you breathe and exhale the ether's light;

your pup growls and craves the fatty mire in my marrow.

Soon you will grow canines sharp enough to speak words that'll cut

through my flesh, the white fleece

of excuses that cover my gray fur,

the child of a Mexican she-wolf and her prodigal mate,

an alpha and beta unfit to keep their pact,

their fangs, whet with any sign of weakness,

raring to bathe their lips with "shut the fuck up"

and "you better not look at me that way when you cry."

These thoughts that make me flee, infested

with visions of you writhing on the floor in anger

as you reveal who *you* are

and my immediate response is to overpower you

with who *I've* been, the dogged spirit

burrowed deep within my heart den

that howls to the moon about the brute,

the brusqueness, the bruxism in its blood:

I won't allow my shadow to be your body,

I'll paw away and bury my pack's shards,

their reflection, my mirror no more.

When you do find your wolf, don't be so quick to kill it,

instead, put your knife away, and listen.

Small Song in My Chest

—after Ross Gay's "Becoming a Horse"

As Mamá Chole's scalding stew and Grandpa Pedro's *fogata*
coddled the strips of tripe into *menudo*,
his 11-month-old cries too boil my guts
and ashen my charcoal hair by the stripe.

Grandma used to tell Grandpa to relax
and not yell at my cousin and me for casting
plastic candy wrappers into his lumber-fueled *lumbre*.

"Just throw them in when he's not looking,"
Grandma Chole used to say. In her mind,
a mischievous child was healthy, playing with the flames, their safe ire—
in spite of Grandpa's nostril-stretching, suspicious sniffs—
was all part of it.

Whatever wrappers survived the night,
my cousin and I used to roll joints from the gunpowder
dissected out of the leftover fireworks from Christmas and New Year's.
We'd take a drag and blow out sparks,
fascinated by the kindle twisted in metallized film
that made our mouths warm,
unafraid of blowing our lips off
or smoking something that wasn't the *real* thing.

Behind the zarape-blotted window
above the mattress where we'd lay to imagine
what our sons would be like when we got to be men,
I remember each exhale filled our eyes
and that dusty room, at dusk, with stars.

As all fire, the one inside my son will burn away
what is no longer needed as the pieces of trash
whose home at the heart of Grandpa's starry *brasero*
forced them to shed their make, name, and whatever else they stood for.
In that resting warmth, nothing remains
but a delicate balance of heat and oxygen,
my skin and his breath on it.

One Day I Too Will Wear Stars

Supermassive black holes could form before galaxies form and act as the seed nuclei for galaxies to form around them, or supermassive black holes can form at the center of galaxies as a result of collisions of many stars and mergers... there is no way to stop the formation of a black hole after you've accrued a certain amount of mass at the center of an active galaxy.
—Ann Wehrle, Observational Astronomer

Colonel Popcorn is my son and commander—nay, prince—
and the popper, when it wafts its plumes of butter and billowed maize
into our inner city realm, is his domain.

He demands, with a maze of grunts and bellows,
the warm puffs detached from their broken shells.
His lips part with trust yet bites down
on my fingers with his seven teeth;
the white flesh melts on his tongue—
a host fed by a guest—
and swallows without question.
The more I give him, the more he wants.

My mother-in-law once told me that when she was a little girl in Jersey,
her grandmother left kernels heating in a pot.
When she returned, the copper grains fired like BBs out of the kettle—
a singularity pushing matter away—
airborne as cabbage whites fresh out their cocoons;
they fell all around them, snowflakes in April.

I posted a picture of my boy with a smirk on his face
and a corny caption underneath, Mom replied on my wall:
"Who taught my baby how to eat *palomitas de maíz*?"
I had no answer because what she asked wasn't a question,
but a star that a black hole had partially or completely torn apart
and was slowly consuming it bit by bit.

The hazard lodged in her tone wasn't due to the inherent choking risk or my gag,
but in someone other than her having communion with her only grandchild,
the kernel of her world— nay, universe.

I reassured her that he was as much hers
as he was his other grandmother's, a sun given to us all.
"But don't you get it?" she replied in a private text,
a secret message rolled up in the craters of a wailing wall.
"The mother and *her* mother are the ones
who shape a child's soul."
She seemed resigned to coming second,
not to my *suegra*, but to her whiteness.

I didn't reply, but wanted to tell her that as the largest black holes
grow faster than their galaxies,
one day, our bodies too will hopefully explode like popcorn
under the immense and wondrous pressure of love,
a heat that will despoil the seed from the dirt, husk, and cob
down to its hull binding it tight only to present its innermost soft,
its sincere, that which holds no fear.

He Sleeps Between Her Breasts

As twilight shows how this sweet corrosion begins to be complete.
—from "How We Made a New Art on Old Ground" by Eavan Boland

I watch with the utmost fear
as our son climbs the bars of his crib,
after the milk is gone, and stands up
for the baby cam only minutes after
my wife laid him in his crib
with a bottle and an *Ave Maria*.

We pick him up and place him in his walker,
he runs unhindered as if on the surface of the moon:
one small step for little man,
one giant leap for her weary mind.

He scuddles to the kitchen
to drum on the trash can— his treasure—
he lifts the lid, pulls on its liner, a big bang.
We run to see what happened:
dust and rubbish spread all over the floor,
my son, the axis of this chaos.

As he rolls around this big crunch
of egg shells and empty popcorn bags,
she walks to him— Mother Earth growing closer to her sun.

They give up the chase, the revolution—
they embrace destruction, each other—
colliding with the inevitable
he sleeps between her breasts.

This nebula of heat,
his body— a jewel no longer
travelling through light and dark and light again—
her body, renewed, as when they were one source,
a single glimmer in space.

From Where I Stand

*So I'm off on the road that I see might be coming
and those dreams that I hold all for this child of mine.*
—The Road by Zero 7

You're not the shoes— the skin or the sole—

the toes, the metatarsals or cuneiforms

or any bone, muscle or sinew in the foot;

you're not the callus, thickening yellow

with every step, stride and shockwave up the tibia,

or the sweat that swaddles the ankle

as a wet nurse who removes the calico from her breast

to suckle another's baby.

You're not the legs—

the splints that tingle down the shins and calves

like a line of ants on a flower's calyx—

or wanderlust, or any impulse or motion that propels

someone from the beginning to the end,

you're not what lies ahead or is left behind,

the light born in the east like a golden chalice

or the darkness that consumes its ambrosia in the west;

you're not the sun that follows the walker
as a leashed dog or the moon that hides in the dark like a cat
only to reveal itself flat and empty
like famine on a plate,
white chipped porcelain in the sky;

you're not hunger or thirst,
the waybread or warm canteen water;
you're not the garbage whirling past,
possessed with the immediacy of someone with somewhere to go;

you're not the trip or the fall, the autumn, the shade
or whatever it is that makes the leaves turn brown and take flight;
no, when someone asks you what it's like to be a parent,
you tell them that it's like being the road—
dust, dirt and everything that's stepped on—
bumps and cracks for stumbling,
suggestions that stray away from the path.

But as the graying ashes remember the heat of the fire,
and the moon nurses the caliches wrought on her flesh by earth,
will I too remember the indentations left behind by his first steps?

His destination, bluntly wedged in clay,
is a cuneiform written in motion and gravity
illegible from where I stand.

Chestnut Sun

Graye rested peacefully in plumage,
wearing Montezuma's headdress underneath the nest
where he had been born only weeks before.
    —Death in Graye

A pair of mourning doves chose to nest
in our hanging mandevillas.
"I think the fat one is the girl," my wife said,
"and the skinny one on the balcony rail is the boy."
We named them Gale and Guy,
as in the French pronunciation, not because he was a "guy" bird.

A few days later, I wasn't surprised to find two eggs
in their nest, perfectly white:
how was Gale able to balance the weight of time,
her empty bones and summer's heat above them?
She somehow knew that the passage of time
would grant her squabs the urge to be born.

When my wife told me she looked fat
and wanted to hire a West Hollywood trainer,
we found out she was pregnant with our second—
the product of her X and mine.

I found the chicks' discarded shells
curled like sardine can lids,
and I thought of my mother and how my son's smile
reminded her of her ex's mischievous grin.

As the squabs grew bigger, they hopped out
of the elevated nest and onto the balcony,
Gale's leaves of absence lingered in the dry air
until one day she never came back.
The squeakers looked like their father,
so we named the smallest one Graye
because he was gray
and the bigger one Ganja
because she was growing like a weed.

My son began to thrash his head against his highchair
whenever I tried to hand-feed him bits of bread,
and bruised his cheek on the side of our coffee table
when he let go of my hands to walk in his body.

One night, our dog chased one of the fledglings
off the balcony, holding the other in its mouth.
"I think Graye was already dead," my wife said.

The chestnut sun peered through Wilshire smog
only to witness gray eyes partially occluded;
I stared at the bird's stiff feathers,
the dirt lacing them, and the emptiness left within.

Luciano's Dream

A wave of anger washed over my bones as the nurse blamed COVID for having to kick me out of the hospital. My unwavering right– a father's enthusiasm to see the ultrasonic echoes of his unborn child– held a damning response tight between its fingers as my son was perched on my left.

I stormed out of the lobby with operatic bravado as the sliding doors parted for me as the Red Sea for Moses and Sunset's naked sidewalks crashed sunlight into my eyes as water columns on Pharaoh's army.

My son and I headed east where a homeless man was pushing a blue sanitation bin in the center divider. The dark gray clothing on his back wasn't the color of his T-shirt, but that of his sweat. He looked over at us– unmoved by the rush of cars on either side– as if my noticing him had rerouted the sweat cascading between his trapezii. "Que onda?" he yelled and waved. I nodded and raised my hand to catch his swell of emotion which rippled through traffic with the sweltering heat.

We came across a French bistro where a French woman served me a French beer: limit one refill. I was hungry, but the Farro salad behind the cool glass didn't look very fresh. I allowed my son to play with the pint's condensation beads as I watched a video my wife had texted me: a close-up of sound-waves, our fetus's heartbeats rolling in and out of focus. When I showed my son the undulating images of his sibling's body, he looked away as if the moon had receded from an eclipse exposing the sun's searing flares. A firetruck roared red in the distance, and my son plugged his ears as it weaved by us, a beast plunging through an ocean of cars and pedestrians.

The reverberating wail flooded my mind with Luciano Pavarotti's voice, and his dream of being able to place his ears in the last seat of a hall just to hear himself sing, to use his ringing vibrato to drown a well of doubt.

I swirled the last swig of beer in my glass and, as it slid swimmingly down my throat, I waived my second serving of the drink and the foam, and motioned my son to wave as the engine floated away in the distance; we waved and waved at it because isn't that all we are, just waves?

Where the Music Comes From

—for Luna

"She moved when I was playing guitar,"
my wife said, her palm flat on the copper strings.
As the life within her rippled beneath her rounded flesh,
I saw how our daughter interpreted the strange sounds
piercing through layers of muscle, fat
and water as melody—
music to be alive to.

I took the guitar from my wife
and plucked a melody from its body,
and I saw how my son slid his hand
into the hole past the vibrations,
the sound, the darkness,
unafraid of what might live in its depths.
He scratched the inner surface and smiled,
relieved to have finally discovered
where the music comes from.

About the Author

Jose Oseguera is the author of the poetry collection *The Milk of Your Blood* (Kelsay Books). His poems have appeared in *Chautauqua, Sonora Review, North Dakota Quarterly, Catamaran* and elsewhere. He was named one of the Sixty Four Best Poets of 2019 by the Black Mountain Press. He was the recipient of the Nancy Dew Taylor Award in 2019 and placed 2nd in the 2020 Hal Prize Contest. His writing has been nominated for the Best of the Net award (2018, twice in 2019) as well as the Pushcart (2018 - 2020) and *Foreword* (2020) Prizes.

homebound
PUBLICATIONS

Homebound Publications is a Trans/Queer Owned publishing house based in the Berkshire Mountains. What began during a brainstorming session in a Boston cafe has become a platform for hundreds of indie authors. More than a company, we are a community of writers and readers exploring the larger questions we face as a global village. We publish full-length works of creative non-fiction and poetry.

homeboundpublications.com

WAYFARER

BASED IN THE BERKSHIRE MOUNTAINS, MASS.

At Wayfarer Books we believe poetry is the language of the earth. We believe words—shaped like rivers through wild places—can change the shape of the world. We publish poets and writers and renegades who stand outside of mainstream culture—poets, essayists, and storytellers whose work might withstand the scrutiny of crows and coyotes, those who are cryptic and floral, the crepuscular, and the queer-at-heart. We are more than just a publisher but a community of writers. Our mission is to produce books that can serve as a compass and map to all wayfarers through wild terrain.

WAYFARERBOOKS.ORG

Milton Keynes UK
Ingram Content Group UK Ltd.
UKHW012250290324
440241UK00004B/278